# God's Other Children; A Spiritual Journey In Gay Life

by
## Tara L. Molina

authorHOUSE™

1663 LIBERTY DRIVE, SUITE 200
BLOOMINGTON, INDIANA 47403
(800) 839-8640
WWW.AUTHORHOUSE.COM

First published by AuthorHouse 08/10/05

ISBN: 1-4208-6535-8 (sc)

Printed in the United States of America
Bloomington, Indiana

This book is printed on acid-free paper.

Dedicated To:
My sister Kira and her family

# Acknowledgments

I would like to thank my baby sister Kira for her support and acceptance in my "coming out" bombshell of 1998, my parents; Robert and Corrouda for at least trying to understand, my friend Toya; just for being my friend, and all my other family members and close friends; (you know who you are.) To my son Francisco and my niece Kirtlynn, I love you guys dearly, and a special thanks to my friend and cover artist, Mr. Rick Brown II.

Most of all thank you God!

Tara L. Molina
April 2005
Pittsburgh, Pennsylvania

# Introduction

This book is intended to inspire gays and lesbians to become secure and confident about their homosexuality, and to quell the fears and anxieties associated with being a Christian as well as a gay person.

My writing is not only geared toward the gay community, but to all of society who needs an understanding of what it's like to be different, unaccepted, scorned and misunderstood.

I hope that after reading this short story based on factual accounts, that everyone will have a better conception of the true meaning of being gay and Christian at the same time.

This is a story about my life's experiences and personal struggles throughout my journey into gay spirituality.

Not one step of the journey was an easy one, until I found the comfort and guidance of Jesus Christ.

# Part 1

God is love; at least that's what the Bible tells us. Over the years I've come to find that this statement is true in every sense of its meaning. It wasn't easy at first, but as time went on I learned to accept the fact that God loved me no matter what. The unconditional, perpetual type of love that a parent has for a child is the exact same love that God has for you and me.

With a good old-fashioned Baptist upbringing in a small rural community, I quickly found out that it wasn't acceptable to be gay. The sneers and mockery of the hick-town homophobes was enough to make even the gayest of gays turn hetero even if only for a short while. The best way to fit into society was to get married and have children whether you wanted to or not. It didn't matter if you were content with your life, as long as society approved then everything was all right.

Different people do different things to gain favor with their beloved society, one might change their hairstyle, another may buy a certain type of car or house that's up to standards for the norm, some would even go as far as to restructure their entire facial appearance through plastic surgery just to fit in, but when you think about it, what does society do for you in return? Most often it ridicules, and oppresses its own. We shouldn't sweat it too much though, because even Jesus' society scorned Him. Nevertheless, I went along with the majority and tried to live my life accordingly. I got married not once, but twice, had one child and fought desperately to remain heterosexual, but I soon realized that heterosexuality was an orientation not a choice. I knew by the time I was eight years old that there was something very 'different' about me. I was raised a spiritual, God-fearing creature of habit just like many others in the world, so I valued the opinions my family and peers. I disregarded my own feelings of attraction to women, thus creating a shy, inhibited child, teenager and then adult. I remember growing up in the late 60's and 70's simply adoring everything that little boys enjoyed. I loved to play rough and tumble with my male friends, we would set out on a hot summer day and climb trees, play touch football, baseball and everything else that young boys played. I always requested toys that were masculine in nature, like G.I. Joe dolls, Mighty Mo dump trucks, and even my bicycle had to be the one with the bar running from the seat to the handlebars, because the bikes without the bar were considered girls' bikes. I even had a crush on my fourth grade teacher Mrs. Ryan, just like all the boys in my class. I'll never forget one day at recess, I was playing touch football with the guys while the little girls played hopscotch and jump rope; all the boys, me included, flocked around Mrs. Ryan to admire her beauty. One of my young male friends said, "Mrs. Ryan you're beautiful, tell your husband I want to marry you."

Mrs. Ryan smiled and thanked him for the compliment. Another little fellow said, "Hey Mrs. Ryan tell your husband that I love you."

Again she smiled, and graciously accepted the adulation. Next however, Mrs. Ryan would not be prepared to hear the subsequent flattery she received. Not understanding the impact of what I was about to tell her, I innocently blurted out, "Mrs. Ryan, tell your husband I'm a 'lesbian'."

Well you can only imagine the look that came over her face. Her pretty brown eyes widened and her jaw almost hit the playground asphalt. She still managed a smile for me, but not until after the initial shock had subsided. I looked around at all the boys, and their faces were repugnantly distorted. I had no idea why everyone was so stunned by what I said. I simply conveyed what I was feeling inside. By now you may be wondering how an eight-year-old knew what the word 'lesbian' meant, well I heard the word from somewhere, I don't recall where, and I looked it up in the dictionary. That's how I knew that it would describe the feelings I had for Mrs. Ryan.

One of my other issues was clothing. Every time my mother would put a dress on me to go to school, I would cry. I didn't like dresses then, and I don't like them now either. When I became a teenager, and my mother suggested wearing makeup, I rebelled and refused to smear my face with cosmetics and look like a girl. Please don't get me wrong, I enjoyed being a girl, but I just could not associate myself with the things that girls were "expected" to do. Now that I'm a grown woman, I still love being a woman; I'm just not too keen on the femininity that goes along with it. Femininity is a wonderful thing, but I like to observe it in other females and not particularly within myself.

I went through a phase while I was married to my first husband, where I did use makeup and wear dresses, but it was merely to please him; in no way was I comfortable in doing so. I often found myself in relationships with men that had no possibility of lasting any reasonable length of time. This wasn't done intentionally, but subconsciously I always seemed to choose men that were fundamentally unavailable. I was in several relationships with married men, and my other choice was men that were much older than myself. I guess I thought this would prevent me from having to seriously commit to any of them.

During my childhood, I was always in church because my parents made me go, but when I was old enough to make my own decisions, I somehow became separated from the religious sect. I suppose in part it had a lot to do with hearing on a weekly basis that God was going to send all homosexuals straight to Hell. I knew that I didn't want to go to Hell, so if I didn't hear about it all the time then maybe I stood a slim chance of spending eternity in God's Paradise. Little did I know back then that through the saving blood of Jesus Christ, my sins were all forgiven; I didn't discover this until much later in my life. So I tarried on over the years living a flagrantly promiscuous lifestyle, jumping from one man to another in search of that heterosexual being that I was "expected" to be.

After a while, I had racked up so many men I couldn't even keep track anymore, nor could I figure out what was missing in my life. I just kept thinking that the more men I slept with, the "straighter" I'd become, but my strategy never panned out.

The era I grew up in was not exactly the safest for sexual promiscuity; by the early 80's a new disease was running rampant throughout the world, Acquired Immune Deficiency Syndrome (AIDS) was killing people by the thousands; today over 20 million have succumbed to this illness, so believe me, I know I was blessed to have escaped it's wrath. I never harbored any guilt about the lives of the men I destroyed; after all, many of them were looking for the same thing I was; sex, and only sex. However, the ones that really cared about me eventually ended up being hurt by my wanton disregard for their feelings. I am remorseful about it now, but at that point in time, I was too much in denial about my own sexuality to care. By no means was my vibrant sexual appetite due to my desire to be with men, it was just my way of trying to prove to society and myself that I couldn't possibly be gay. The question most often posed to me by people that know my situation is, "How could you be gay when you were married twice and have a child? You obviously have been intimate with men."

My reply is simply this; "I basically used men as a shield to hide my gayness."

Along with the countless men that unknowingly aided in my charade, I found a comforting solace in the use of illicit drugs. Starting in my teenage years, marijuana and alcohol were my drugs of choice. I smoked pot almost every day, and drank anything that I could get my hands on. One time I put away nearly a half pint of 151 proof Purple Label Ron Rico rum, and several bottles of Mickey's Malt Liquor. I was eighteen at the time, and never in my life had I ever been so sick. All I can remember is fading in and out of consciousness, and trying to watch The Jefferson's on my grandmother's TV. I thank God for having been overweight all my life because I believe to this day that that is why I didn't die from alcohol poisoning. I had just enough extra weight on me to absorb the toxic amount that I drank. Afterwards, I moved on to bigger, more powerful drugs, and experimented with them for years. I mistakenly believed that they were helping me cope with my confusion and denial; I was once again blessed to escape unscathed.

By the time I left home and moved away with my first husband, a hotheaded Puerto Rican, I started to turn in the right direction. My husband was arrested, and sentenced to one year in the county jail for selling marijuana, and I decided at that time I should join a church. I convinced my husband to get baptized with me and start attending services. We did, but only for a short time. When he was released from jail, Satan stepped in and sidetracked our lives right back to the drug scene. My husband was an abusive womanizer, which didn't help my situation at all. I spent almost seven years running from him in order to save my life. I was subjected to severe physical, psychological and verbal abuse throughout my entire marriage. I had never been abused before that. Many professionals that try to determine reasons why people are gay, very often blame it on abusive relationships, lack of a mother or father figure in the home, incest, molestation or rape. This may be the cause for some, but in my case, none of these terrible things ever happened to me. The abuse I suffered at the hands of my husband came long after my first fleeting thought of being with a woman. Two of the worst beatings I endured came when my husband caught me reading the Vanessa Williams issue of Playboy one too many times; and the other was when I told him that I paid him back for cheating on me by having an affair of my own with his brother. For those of you who are not familiar with Vanessa Williams, she was the first African American woman to become Miss America, and was subsequently dethroned for posing nude with another woman in several precarious positions in the 'men's' entertainment magazine. The Playboy incident left me with a shiner that I had to cover with makeup and sunglasses for a week, and the affair caused my husband to slap me so hard on the side of my face that my eardrum ruptured requiring an agonizing patch repair job by an otologist. It took three weeks before I could hear again; I was beginning to think that my ear would not regain its audibility. Since I was very young and naïve, I believed that I deserved what I got. I know now that no matter what you do wrong, it's no cause for someone to hit you. All of the other battering I received was over little or nothing. I never mentioned a word to my family about the abuse because of the shame that came along with it. It's not easy to tell someone that you're getting the life beat out of you on a regular basis.

There were many separations during this marriage, it seemed like every six months my husband was packing up everything, including the waterbed, and moving out. The separations never lasted long; within the first week apart he would always call up begging for me to take him back. Foolishly, I did every time, mainly for the sake of our child. Finally, the last time he decide to move out, I recall coming home from work and seeing the old familiar sight of the hose hanging from the bedroom window draining the waterbed so he could take it with him. By this point I was fed up, so I went into the house, and after making sure he was not there, I took a straight pin and poked several hundred holes into the mattress. To his surprise, when he moved into his new apartment and tried to refill the waterbed, it turned into a beautiful fountain of water spewing all over his lovely new abode. Also to his dismay, when he called me in one week asking to come home, I flatly replied, "No." It took all I had within me to refuse, but I held firm to my decision. One day he showed up at my front door with a dozen roses and tears in his eyes, and tried once again to make me reconsider. This was the first time I remember praying aloud to God to help me not take him back. An overwhelming feeling of power and strength took over inside me, and I closed the door in his face forever. Within in the next six months, we were officially divorced.

I continued on my downward spiral with men and drugs, still not able to face the demons of guilt and refutation. I added many more victims to my wall of shame and deceit. I kept telling myself that one day I would be honest with the next man that I met and just tell him that I could not enter into a relationship with him because I'd rather be with a woman, but each time I tried, I remembered the look of repulsion on my classmates' faces when I uttered, "Tell your husband I'm a lesbian," like I was giving the time of day. Also reverberating in my head was that Baptist minister from years ago claiming homosexuality was a sin before God, and the whispered insults about the gay people who lived in our town by many of my friends and family members. Oddly enough most of the gay people were my family members. As I recall, on my mother's side of the family there was at least one gay child per every cousin that my mother had. This is not an exaggeration, and it's what makes me believe that homosexuality is indeed hereditary. It's like inheriting a one blue eye one green eye trait, or a curly hair gene; it just can't be helped. Conservative Christians would beg to differ with me, but since I've lived it, I can be a witness that it can and does happen.

In 1990, I decided to give marriage another try; maybe now would be the time that I would turn heterosexual. Well, that union lasted all of six months. I married on a whim because I felt the longer I was single the more people would think something was wrong with me. So I leaped headfirst into another bad situation by marrying an alcoholic. Yes of course I was still a big drinker also, but I was not an alcoholic by far. This particular man drank beer for breakfast, lunch, dinner, and midnight snack. He was a red-faced Irishman with a raging temper, but thankfully he never laid a hand on me. There was some verbal abuse, and ethnic intimidation because when he drank he tended to forget he was married to a black woman, and the racial slurs would flow freely. It took no time at all to end this fluke of a marriage.

The next big mistake I made was one year later. I stumbled into a relationship with a married man; "there would be no danger here", I thought, because he was already committed to someone else. I was "safe" again. The attraction for me was the fact that he was eighteen years older than me, and a thin whisp of a man, with long flowing hair, and effeminate demeanor. At times he acted more feminine than I did; this was not a difficult task to accomplish as it was. His attitude was passive, and he was very sensitive, just like a woman would be. We did fall in love, and he decided to leave his wife; this is where the trouble began. She was not about to let us be together without putting up a good fight. The more she fought, the more confused he became about leaving her. It got to the point where he was torn between her and me. This tug-of-war struggle went on for six years. There were times that he would disappear from the house we shared and return to his wife, but it was never for very long; he always came back to me. During the relationship he made false promises that he was going to divorce her so we could be married, but I knew deep inside that this would never happen; I'm not even sure if I wanted it to. His wife and I continued to battle back and forth until one day I told this man he would have to make a decision because I couldn't take it anymore. His wife was a successful businesswoman with lots of money, and that I could not compete with. She made him an offer to move out of state with her and she would take care of him for the rest of his life.

As we sat on the couch one evening, I told him with the utmost sincerity, which he mistook for a joke that if he and I ever split up my next relationship would be with a woman. He laughed it off, but I had never been more serious. I couldn't believe that I had finally found the courage to let the thought in mind exit through my mouth. I had never confessed this to anyone before. He continued to play both ends to the middle, and I upheld my end of the bargain. I had befriended a woman in my bowling league that I knew was a lesbian; I was attracted to her from the very start. We became closer and I began to confide in her about my situation. Before long I was completely renewed; this woman and I embarked on a mission to be together. As far as my man knew, the woman was just a "friend" of mine, but in all essence it was much more than that. I would bring her home on occasion after drinking and bowling together, and we would retire to an upstairs bedroom while my man slept on the couch. He had made this choice months before to no longer share a bed with me; he would never tell me why, no matter how many times I asked. We hadn't made love for almost a year. When he started to notice that my "friend" was coming home with me more often, he began to ask questions. He wanted to know why I always went upstairs with her and left him sleeping on the couch. I explained that since he longer used our bed then I might as well sleep with my "friend". He still didn't grasp the concept that I wasn't just sleeping with her; there was more going on behind the closed door. At last he panicked, and began to put it all together. He remembered my comment about being with a woman after him, and suddenly he wanted to do everything right. He was now ready to get his divorce and start sleeping in bed with me again, but by now there was no turning back for me. I advised him that he should go back to his wife and accept her offer to move out of state. It took a while for it to sink in, but he eventually moved out and went back to his wife. Several years later tragedy struck, and my ex-boyfriend's wife committed suicide on Memorial Day of 2003, two months later he called me out of the blue, and told me that he still loved me very much and wanted us to get back together. I told him that nothing had changed; I was still living my newfound life, and we could remain friends. He thanked me for offering to be his friend, told me to take care, and that he would always love me. He then hung up the phone. One week later I received a call from a mutual friend telling me that my ex-boyfriend's partially decomposed body was found in his home with a self-inflicted gunshot wound to the head. I was devastated. It took a while for me to realize that I was not to blame; even if I had agreed to resume our relationship, the depression he suffered over the loss of his wife would have still driven him to suicide. The only difference may have been that I would have most likely discovered his body.

As for me though I was finally free, completely out of the closet that had held me captive for twenty-seven years. The strife and turmoil that I suffered was over at last. The stranglehold of guilt, doubt, denial, and betrayal was gone; I could breathe easily. I no longer felt like a liar and a 'Jezebel'. The fling between the woman from my bowling league and myself ended after four months, but we both knew that it would; we were never really trying to have a lasting relationship. For me it was my stepping-stone into the life that I knew I belonged. I was never a heterosexual, I only played the role. I must admit I played it well, and deserved an Academy Award for being able to do so. The drugs and the promiscuity went out with the deceit; I was clean now. The next thing I had to do was find all the people that I had deceived and let them know who I really was. "Coming Out" to everybody was not easy, but I had to confess. I first told my family, and then a few select friends. What really shocked me is that most of them told me they were not surprised. They knew all along that I was "different", but they too were in denial just as I was.

Later on I met a young lady and fell in love with her; we were together for a total of three years. I was a believer in God, but she was not. Her family was Atheist, and she was raised to believe that there was no God. This may sound strange to you, but I'm a firm believer that one can be Christian and gay at the same time, so I promptly introduced my girlfriend to God's word, and after reading some Scriptures she asked me how she could become a Christian too. Upon telling her that all she needed to do was to confess her sins, and believe that Jesus is the Son of God who died on The Cross for our sins and rose again, I realized that I hadn't confessed to God my sin of being deceitful to Him all my life. I wasn't confessing the fact that I was gay, God already knew that; He created me. Therefore I didn't feel as though it was a sin to be gay, at least not anymore. I truly felt in my heart that my biggest sin was being a deceiver, not being true to God or myself by trying to hide who I was for so long.

My girl and I set out to find an accepting church that we could join and become closer to God. We found a liberal Presbyterian church that was open and welcoming to the gay community. A church that would not close it's doors to a gay couple and try to prevent them from seeking the word of God. We became members of that church, and I converted from Baptist to Presbyterian, and my girl converted from Atheist to Christian. I was ecstatic that I played a role in leading a soul to Christ.

We worshipped and fellowshipped regularly; even attending church on Wednesday nights as well as Sunday mornings. I felt fantastic for the first time in my life. I could finally feel God's presence in all aspects; I couldn't find the words to describe my joy. The conservative Christians say that it was the Devil deceiving me into believing that God had accepted me, but there is no way that the Devil would make someone feel so good about God. Satan works the opposite way; he tries to steal our joy in the Lord, not build it up. I have no reason to lie to you about the way I felt when I reconnected with The Savior; I began to notice drastic changes in my life, all for the good.

After getting settled into our new church, my girl and I took advantage of the Civil Union agreement offered by the state of Vermont. We hopped into the car and drove ten hours from Pennsylvania to Vermont, and were united in a Civil Union ceremony. When we came back home we made arrangements for a Holy Union to be conducted at our church. The pastor was delighted to officiate at the ceremony; as far as we were concerned we became wife and wife before God and witnesses that day. We continued

living life as any regular married couple would; we got more involved in our church, serving on the usher board and doing other volunteer work; everything flowed smoothly for the next couple of years, and then some problems began to erupt.

My wife wasn't much of a worker outside of the home, but she had promised over the years that she would get a job and help me to make ends meet. I was a struggling taxicab driver because my business had declined drastically after the 911 terrorist attack on the US. Money just wasn't coming in fast enough anymore, so I really needed my wife to get serious about earning money to help our financial situation. When she kept putting off the effort to look for gainful employment, our relationship started to falter. We began bickering more often, and I became extremely stressed out. For reasons unknown, my wife slipped into a bout of major depression, thus adding more strain on our union. We attended counseling sessions together to help bring her out of the depression and to strengthen our relationship, but even though we were committed to the therapy, it didn't help our circumstances. The marriage started to deteriorate even more, and my wife fell back into an old drug habit that she had given up several years before we met; this was the last straw for me. She started stealing money from my family and me to support her resurrected crack habit, and I refused to go any further with her and our relationship. We parted ways, but remained civil; she moved to the Carolinas with her family, and tried to pull her life back together there. I never thought that being with a woman would be easier than being with a man; I knew that it would not guarantee a lasting relationship.

Some of my straight friends ask me would I have stayed married to a man if the relationship didn't fail for other reasons. I can honestly answer, "No." Because I was destined to be with a woman, it's just how I was born, and I know that at any given time during either of my marriages to men, I would have eventually sought the touch of a woman.

Most likely I would have been labeled an adulterer because I know I would have ended up being unfaithful. I believe my friends were under the assumption that once I got into a relationship with a woman then it would never fail; this of course is an illogical supposition. All relationships are subject to failure; it takes a tremendous effort to make one work. God knows I'm still trying.

After the breakup with my wife, I eased my way back into the dating scene, taking very careful steps so I would not make another mistake. I was going to take my time and really get to know the next woman that I met. What I found out is that women are not much different than men. Aside from women being more loyal and sensitive than their male counterparts, everything else is pretty much the same. Women tend to gravitate toward prospective partners that are just plain "no good", and men are the same way. They say they want someone who will respect them and treat them right, but when you grant this request, they pull away and get involved with just the opposite. The more attention you give to them, the less they give to you, but the moment you stop giving them the time of day, they want to follow you to the ends of the Earth. I don't know if I'll ever understand the reasoning behind this.

One woman in particular comes to mind when I think of the 'You want me so I don't want you syndrome'. I met this woman through a mutual friend, and at first we were very attracted to each other. We exchanged phone numbers and talked for hours almost every day of the week. We dated off and on, and really enjoyed each other's company. As we got closer to starting a relationship, all of sudden she got cold feet and broke camp. I kept trying to reel her back in, but she fought me off like a big fish. I grew weary trying to convince her that I was a good Christian woman that would never hurt her, and I gave up. We remained friends for several years, and one day out of nowhere she decides that she wants to rekindle what we had, and try to do the relationship thing. Well by now I had lost all interest in being with her that way, so I declined. I guess my declination went right over her head; I get a phone call every few months from her trying to win me back.

Trying to figure women out is not always easy. My sister tells me it's because I have more of a male thinking pattern, so she tries to school me on the way a feminine brain works. I am learning slowly but surely. What we're working on right now is why women will lure you into a relationship, steal your heart and then dump you without reason. This happened to me last year. I met a woman online who lived five hours from my hometown. We fell for each other instantly. Within a week's time she came to visit me and we really hit it off. Every two weeks she would come to my house and spend the weekend with me. She was in school working on her Master's Degree and made plans to move to Pennsylvania with me when she graduated. We made long-term plans for the future, including marriage and artificial insemination for her. I sincerely believed she would be the one that I would spend the rest of my life with. She was twelve years younger than me, and had some issues because her family was totally against her sexual orientation. Her mother was a Baptist minister, and her father who passed away during our six-month relationship was borderline homophobic. In spite of that, everything seemed to be going well for us. We talked on the phone one night and she was acting normal, she told me she loved me before we hung up. The next morning I awaited her wakeup call as I always did; when my phone rang she sounded a little strange to me. I asked her what was wrong, and she matter-of-factly told me that she could no longer be in a relationship with me. I thought I was dreaming. I couldn't believe my own ears; how could this be? I began to laugh because now I was thinking it was a joke, but she sternly said, "I'm for real, I can't see you anymore. Goodbye."

My heart started to pound, and slowly rose into my throat. I was devastated; she gave no warning, no reason. I was basically left to try and figure out why on my own. I ended up attributing it to her family's pressure; especially her mother the preacher, that would tell her that the lifestyle she lived would send her to Hell. There was nothing else that I could conceive for the cause of this breakup.

The pressure. It's awful, the pressure that the gay community as a whole has to endure. It's almost as if we're outcasts of society who get no respect and no rights as human beings. Even right down to some of the so-called Christian people who use God's Word as a weapon to deter homosexuals from coming to Jesus. Don't these so-called Christians know that they are causing gays to turn away from God rather than leading us to Him? What kind of true Christian would do that? They just don't stop to realize what God will think of them on Judgment Day. They're so busy doing God's job of condemning us that they don't even look in the mirror at themselves.

If the conservative Christians could just take the time to hear some of the stories of gay people, maybe they would begin to understand us a little better. They are all so ready to jump to conclusions that all gays are promiscuous pedophiles with an agenda to turn the whole world gay. This is absurd. We hear more stories in the news about Catholic priests molesting children than gay people molesting them; this is an unfortunate known fact. To me it is so blatantly obvious that an effeminate man is not merely putting on a show and acting feminine purposely. It seems that sooner or later he would forget and start acting masculine; one can only put on a performance for a short period of time before reverting back to their normal characteristics. Most of the feminine gay men that I know have been this way since they were young boys. Again I'll say that many mental health professionals attribute this to molestation or male figure abandonment, of course this is a possibility, but what about those young feminine boys who had a stable father figure and were never molested? Isn't it remotely possible that God created them this way?

I believe God gave us proof to the actuality that some women have stronger male traits causing lesbianism, and some men have stronger female traits triggering homosexuality, when he created hermaphrodites. Hermaphrodites are real human beings that are both male and female; that alone, should be enough evidence from God that it is more than possible for someone to be born gay. If the genes within a hermaphrodite can become so crossed while inside the womb that the child can have a penis and a vagina, then why can't the same hold true for homosexuals? Our genetics can crisscross as well, thus determining our sexual orientation.

I'm sure hermaphrodites must have a tougher life than gays because most of the time at birth, someone decides what sex the child is going to be. Well what happens if the well-meaning parent or doctor chooses the wrong sex? Why don't they just leave them alone and let them decide what they want to be when the time is right? Then again, if they came into the world with dual sexual body parts then that must have been what God wanted. Just leave it alone altogether.

I was ever so close to letting our conservative Christian society keep me away from God with their constant Bible bashing techniques. The way they will pull a verse from God's word and try to intimidate gays into believing that homosexuality is the worst sin that can be committed, and is an abomination before God. I'm glad I finally realized that I have to live and die for myself, and if I'm going to go to Hell, it will be over something I did, and not something that the so-called Christians forced me into.

This brings me to another issue of how the Bible has been translated by man. Could it be because of man's translation of the Bible that homosexuality was deemed immoral? Did God say that, or did man decide that God said that? I'm not trying to doubt God's word, but how did the gang raping of the angels in Sodom and Gomorrah become translated into "homosexuality"? Now I'm sure that the conformists will throw (Leviticus 18:22) in my face, where it clearly states that: *"You shall not lie with a male as one lies with a female; it is an abomination"*, but to that I'll respond, why did God not go on to further iterate that a woman should also not lie with a woman as she would a man? Nowhere does the Bible say this. Instead God goes on to say that: *"A woman should not stand before an animal to mate with it; it is a perversion"*, (Leviticus 18:23)

The Law of the Bible tells us that there are so many things that are abominations before God, such as rounding the edges of your hair, shaving off your beard, tattoos, eating unclean foods, etc; the list goes on and on, but all these things seem to have been done away with in the New Testament after the birth of our Savior Jesus Christ who said absolutely nothing regarding homosexuality in His teachings; it would appear to me that He would have said something about it if it was as immoral as we are led to believe. Nevertheless, conformists continue to agree that of all abominations, "homosexuality" is the greatest of all.

All the things we read in the Bible have been translated hundreds of times over the ages by man. We have no way of knowing what was taken away from or added to God's original word. So therefore, how do we know what part of the Bible to believe? I think the answer is simple; if it sounds godly then it's all right to believe it. Let's face it; there are some parts of the Bible that do not sound very godly. Slavery is just one of the things that one would think God would not tolerate; yet and still our forefathers used these slavery passages to justify holding other human beings in bondage and using them as slaves. Another is the obvious adultery and incest that took place throughout the Bible. The story of Abraham, Sarah, and Hagar the concubine, is a perfect example of the adultery that I'm speaking of. Sarah, who was barren, persuaded Abraham, her husband to commit adultery by having relations with Hagar so that she and Abraham could have a child. This was certainly an ungodly proposition. As far as incest is concerned, are we supposed to assume that Adam and Eve, the first human beings created by God, were somehow a party to it? They had two children, Cain and Abel, both of them males. Since Cain and Abel each had children of their own, are we to assume that Eve was the mother of their children? The Bible does not mention who bore their offspring. Did "man" intentionally leave this information out of the Good Book to make us think immorally by assuming incest? Maybe God created another whole family apart from Adam and Eve, but if He did, why was it left out of the Bible?

Another thing that perplexes me is how Christians view Christ's teachings on divorce. Jesus plainly states that save for the reason of adultery, married couples should not divorce one another, and if a man does divorce his wife and she marries someone else, then it causes the person whom she marries to commit adultery. (Matthew 19:9) Why then are now so many divorces for reasons other than infidelity that Christians seem to condone without batting an eye? The concern for keeping a marriage together based on the Bible's values should be treated with the same concern that the conservatives have regarding homosexual relationships; no one seems to want to focus on this issue, just the issues surrounding the homosexual "agenda". Conservative Christians really should apply their time and energy on the staggering divorce statistics rather than using the Bible to bash gays.

Lastly, I'm disturbed by the verses pertaining to women submitting unto men. The Bible makes it sound as though women are second-class citizens lacking human rights, that must obey men and submit to them at will. This makes it seem that women were not created as equals. Is this really what God intended? Society seems so ready to condone adultery, incest and submission simply because it is so rampant in the Bible.

I love to read God's word, and I hope that my views regarding the Bible's authenticity are not taken out of context; I do believe that a vast majority of the Bible is the true word of Almighty God. All I'm really trying to say here is that it disheartens me somewhat to know that I may not be getting the whole story, or that some of it is what "man" wanted it to be.

I personally believe that one of the biggest sins is for people who call themselves Christians to use the Bible to bash others with what they believe is their assignment to deliver God's message. Most of the time they don't even know what God's message is. Take for instance the preachers who sermonize more about homosexuality than they do about Christ dying for our sins. I watch a lot of Christian programs on television, and the thing I hear the most from televangelists is regarding homosexuality. Of all the things that need to be addressed, and prayed over, they seem to focus only on the gay community. It's almost like an obsession. Rarely do I hear them talk about gambling, adultery, psychics, horoscopes, and all the other things that God says we should not do; they are just fixated by homosexuals. Some of them are worse than others, and some do not even bring up the subject. It's hard to fathom that some of these televangelists don't have a gay person within their family; I'm sure they are out there. Even the size of the congregations that flock to hear these ministers tells me that there must be at least one gay person amongst them. I don't think these preachers take this into consideration when they start gay bashing in front of hundreds of people.

It really irks me when I hear the gay rights movement referred to as the "homosexual agenda". The Rev. Pat Robertson and Focus on the Family use this term very loosely. An agenda is a plan, scheme, or a plot, none of which gay people are trying to achieve. We are not scheming to turn all of America gay, nor are we planning to destroy family values. In my opinion, the "agenda" lies within the conservative Christian circle as they plan, scheme, and plot to destroy a part of society that God has created; the homosexual.

I know one pastor in particular from my old hometown that went to a church to preach as a visitor; and knowing way ahead of time that the organist and one of the choir members were a lesbian couple, he prepared his sermon to deliberately try and demoralize these two women. He preached on the immorality of homosexuality, and how all gays would burn in Hell for eternity. These ladies were friends of mine, and I know that their faith in God would not allow them to be discouraged by this. I also know that they were not ashamed because their church had already accepted them for who they were, and even more important than that, God accepted them. These ladies were prominent figures in their church; volunteering their time and talents to serve a God they loved. This minister had no right to single them out and try to ruin their reputation; this is a good example of an "agenda". However, that's another wonderful thing about God, when you serve and love Him, no one can turn Him against you; not even a preacher with a blatant "agenda".

# Part 2

Marriage: The union between a "man" and a "woman"? Our government that is all about not mixing church and state, is the same government that makes us "swear to tell the truth, the whole truth and nothing but the truth, so help you God", prints currency with the "In God We Trust" logo, and vehemently rallies to prevent gays from getting married. Regardless of the lopsided contradictions, the lame excuse that they're using for the gay marriage issue is that it would threaten "traditional" marriage. I sit scratching my head and pondering how the government, as well as some religions came to this absurd conclusion. To me, traditional marriages became threatened right around the baby boomers era; climbing divorce rates started to happen long before gay people ever thought about legally obtaining a marriage license.

God created marriage, and yes He did say that a "man" and a "woman" would be joined together to become one, but if two people are in love and want to spend the rest of their lives together, I can't see how God would not bless such a union built on love. It seems that it would be more acceptable for two men or two women to be married, rather than having a man and a woman living together in "sin", this is only my opinion. Not allowing gays the privilege of God's gift of holy matrimony forces us to have to live in "sin" with our partners.

One asinine statement from a government official was that gay marriage would cause straight people to turn gay so that they could marry someone of the same sex. First of all, being gay is not contagious. Therefore, if I'm gay, that doesn't mean if someone comes into contact with me they will also become gay. We as the gay community are not trying to recruit people to become homosexuals; all we asked for was the equal right to be married to each other. I can only conclude that there is some level of fear involved in the government's decision to ban gay unions. I don't know what they're afraid of, but the reasons they are giving are utterly ridiculous. If they think it is ethically wrong, they should let the individuals involved worry about their own immorality. It is not the government's place to pry into the private lives of United States citizens.

The Pennsylvania state senator who proclaimed that allowing gay marriage would be akin to legalizing incest, bestiality, pedophilia and bigamy was obviously expressing his own moronic ignorance regarding what homosexuality really is. He must not have realized that there are many more straight people involved in these carnal acts than gays. To be gay doesn't mean that one would have sex with a family member, an animal, a child or have multiple spouses. It really doesn't amount to sex at all. Homosexuality is the attraction for someone of the same sex, meaning that one could have same sex desires and never even have sexual relations. It is merely an attraction.

Another harebrained excuse for denying our rights for marriage is that it would cause a dysfunction of family values. What about all the other issues that cause family dysfunction, such as single parent homes, orphaned children, and the parents who teach their children to hate?

A mother and a father teaching a child to be racist, is far worse than a lesbian or gay couple raising a child together without hatred. Our society's way of thinking is so out of kilter that it's almost disgusting. It would rather see a homeless child living in a shelter, rather than being adopted by a gay couple that could raise the child and provide the love and caring that it needs. A child living with two gay parents does not mean that the child would grow up to be gay; it just doesn't happen that way. I have several lesbian and gay friends raising children, and those kids are very heterosexual. Homosexuality is not a learned behavior, but hatred and bigotry most certainly are.

The final thing that comes to mind regarding our fine government's homophobia is how gay marriage would inhibit procreation. All I can say to this is, as long as there are women in the world, there will always be a way to reproduce. I guess it was never taken into consideration that there are many married hetero couples that don't even want to have children. Doesn't that hinder procreation as well? If a gay couple, male or female has the desire to have children, there is always a way to accomplish this. Lesbians have the option of artificial insemination, and gay men have the option of recruiting a surrogate. Grant it, these are not the "traditional" ways of reproduction, but neither is fertility medication that infertile couples rely on to have children.

It would be a blessing if the government would stick its nose back into the White House, and leave the sanctity of marriage to God. I also pray that one-day our nation's leaders will have a change of heart and see that there really is no harm in allowing two people who love each other and want to spend their lives together to marry.

I'll be the first to admit that I've come a long way in my spiritual journey with Christ since my early years of being dragged, kicking and screaming to my Baptist church with my parents, and now, eagerly awaiting the arrival of

Sunday mornings so I can willingly attend church to honor God with the praise and gratitude He deserves. I've noticed so many changes in my life since "coming out" of the old proverbial closet. God has moved in my life and guided me through some major decisions by way of the Holy Spirit; I can honestly say that I actually know when God is speaking to me now. The Holy Spirit has taught me how to pray in order to receive God's blessings, and He has also showed me how to remain "quiet" so that I can be more receptive when God speaks to me. I have found that if all you do is pray, pray, pray, then you might miss the message that God is sending to you. The best thing to do is pray for a little while then sit back quietly and say nothing. You might ask, how do I know when God tells me something? Well, it's not easy to figure out at first, but when you become spiritually connected with God, His message reveals itself quite clearly. For instance, the things that some people chalk up to being a mere coincidence are actually signs from God. There is no such thing as coincidence, chance, or luck within the spiritual realm of The Lord; every incident that takes place is in one way or another connected to God. It doesn't matter if the circumstance is good or bad; God always plays a major role in it. I have some friends who are nonbelievers that I try to convince that "*Jesus is way, the truth and life*", as He said himself in (John 14:6) but they remain blinded and unwilling to surrender their lives to Him. Instead they question me about why God allows bad things to happen, and if He really is God then why doesn't He do something about them. I always respond with (Romans 8:28) *"God causes 'ALL' things to work together for good to those who love Him, and to those who are called according to His purpose"*. This seems to be the best answer to their question because in every bad circumstance, there is always something good that can be learned from it. It may take some time to realize what the good things are, but since

God said that "ALL" things work together for good, then it's up to us to discern what they are; you can believe that if you put God in the center of your life, He will help you see the good within the bad. A certain circumstance may be the worst thing you've ever experienced, but with faith and trust in God you'll always be able to think of something that would have been even more tragic than what occurred in your life.

One of my non-believing friends became separated from God when her three-year old child died suddenly; she has never forgiven Him for taking her little girl away. Whenever I witness to her about the goodness of God, she always reminds me that He let her child die. I always remind her that God let His own child die also, and it was for the sake of all His other children. After nineteen years my friend is still trying to figure out why God did this to her, but the one thing she doesn't understand is that God doesn't have to seek permission from us to carryout His will. Maybe God foresaw something that this little child would have suffered through later in life and saw fit to remove her from it before having to endure it. It's hard to say, but we know since this unfortunate thing happened that it was indeed God's will for it to take place.

There are so many things that God does for us that we take for granted. Waking up in the morning in good health is not something we do for ourselves; it is something that God wills for us. Having breakfast on the table is not of our own doing, but is provided by God. Leaving our homes and arriving safely at work is not accomplished by our skillful driving techniques, but is the will of God to protect us. He is with us everywhere, and we should always be everywhere with Him. It doesn't matter if you're driving down a busy highway, taking a jog in the park, going on a job interview, or even taking a restroom break, God should always be in your heart. I don't know what I would have done if God had not pulled me from the stranglehold of deception so that I could live freely without shame and guilt.

Before admitting to God and myself that I was a lesbian, I used to pray for Him to change me, to make me heterosexual. My gayness could not possibly be a choice; no one would choose a lifestyle that would bring scorn and ridicule upon one's self. It just so happened that it was not God's will to make me "straight". He obviously has a plan and a purpose for me just the way I am. All I know is that I'm grateful to Him for saving me. I want to do all I can for God, but sometimes I feel like I'm not doing enough; I know there will never be a way that I can repay Him for all that He's done, but all I can do for now is continue to praise Him and try to live my life to glorify His name.

Some of you may be wondering how a lesbian can glorify the name of God; well, if being born a homosexual is really a sin, then it would be no different than how a murderer, a thief, a liar, a drunkard or any other sinner would glorify God if they consider themselves Christians. Since there is no one without sin then it must be accurate to say that all Christians are sinners. It doesn't matter what your transgression is we are all still sinners. Those who think they are without sin are actually committing a sin with that line of thinking as well. The Christians that do the finger pointing and gossiping about homosexuals seem to think that they will not go to Hell on Judgment Day because they are heterosexual; I believe they have forgotten about the other sins they may be guilty of committing. For example, I remember attending one Sunday morning service, and one of our transgendered fellow parishioners was serving as usher. It was time to pass the collection plate for tithes, and the usher proudly served "her" God by collecting the money in "her" assigned section of the pews. I couldn't help but notice an older heterosexual couple gawking ignorantly at the usher. I saw the man lean over to his wife and mouth the words, "That's a man," and then start to snicker. The wife made sure she paid closer attention to God's servant so that she too could mock the usher behind "her" back. Now this is the kind of action that is labeled a sin. This couple was not doing anything to glorify God, but they had the audacity to sit there in church and ridicule a transgendered man who was devoting his life to serving a God that he obviously loved. I certainly don't consider what the elderly couple did to be very Christ-like, and since God is always watching what we do, I hardly believe that He took very kindly to it either. The God that I worship would not care one way or the other that the woman who was collecting tithes for God's storehouse was actually a man in women's clothing. For me, the transgendered man was more of a Christian than the couple who made fun of him.

The same goes for ministers who will not welcome a homosexual into their church, and churches that defrock gay clergymen, or ban them completely from preaching and ordination. I will however, give credit where it is due. My old Baptist church that used to demoralize anyone that it thought had a hint of homosexual tendencies is no longer practicing those narrow-minded ethics. The church recently obtained a new pastor, and he is the epitome of what Christianity is supposed to be. The man is truly an angel. He has the type of understanding and compassion that all ministers should have.

Even during one of our church meetings, a long standing member boldly proclaimed that she once said under no circumstance would she ever leave the church, but if anyone tried to ban gays and lesbians from seeking Christ at our church by adding a clause to the bylaws to do such a thing, she would be the first one to walk away in shame of ever having been a member. This elderly woman deserved kudos and huge round of applause for having the courage to speak her mind the way she did.

I had the privilege of being invited back to my old church by my sister, and I was extremely happy that I went. The pastor and the congregation made my homecoming an enjoyable experience. So in essence, it is possible for old dogs to be capable of new tricks, and all for the glory of God. With the changes that my Baptist church was willing to make to be more accepting of God's other children, I am now dividing my time between two houses of worship.

The church should be a place where all can feel welcome and secure, but unfortunately with the mindset of many Christians, the doors of our churches are nailed shut to the gay community. This is why I think there are so many non-believing gays and lesbians in the world today. When a particular group of citizens is ostracized, and derided by people that claim to be Christians, and are told that God doesn't love them, then how could a homosexual believe in God. We are all made in the likeness of God, and His love is supposed to be displayed through us, so if the majority of heterosexual Christians go around condemning gays, then it's understandable why some of us in the gay community would ultimately "hate" God. The Lord's own people are setting a bad example of who He really is. If all Christians would come together and love one another no matter what, then maybe our fellow homosexuals would begin to feel God's love.

I tend to believe that this lack of Christian love and acceptance is partially to blame for the disproportionate amount of alcoholic and drug addicted gays in America; they feel that this is their only escape. Our churches need to welcome members of the gay society and preach about God's love in such a way His other children will know that He is a merciful, gracious, and loving Father who will guide and protect His people like a shepherd watching over his flock. I pray that unaccepting Christians will stop defaming God's character and start setting an example of what He really stands for... Love.

I'm sure it pains God when He sees the outcome of what some of His heterosexual children are doing to His homosexual children. I will liken this to a parent having one child who is beautiful, healthy, and smart, and another that is sickly, unintelligent and homely. The parent would not tolerate the fortunate child mistreating or not accepting its unfortunate sibling, so why would one suppose that God would tolerate the abuse of one of His children by the other? It's time to start gaining some acceptance

for people that are different, and stop shunning the varieties of human beings that God has created.

Another baffling dilemma that I've experienced in regards to acceptance is happening right inside the gay community itself. When it comes down to dating and relationships, I've found that a majority of Caucasian gays have a big problem with dating outside of their own race. Of course there are some African Americans who feel the same way, but it's not to the same degree as whites. Since we as gay people are a minority to begin with, you would think that we would all stick together and forget about prejudice. Unfortunately, this is not the case. I have heard many white gay men and women say that they, under no circumstance would date a black person, and vice versa. This is about the craziest thing I have ever heard. We experience such extreme prejudice as it is already; why on Earth are we destroying each other with issues regarding the color of one's skin?

Personally, there was no tolerance for discrimination in my family; I was raised to believe that all people were created equal in the sight of God. So I just can't fathom how gay people could discriminate against each other just because one of them is of another race. We're all gay for

God's sake; we should come together and see only that part of the issue.

When I first "came out", I naively thought that this is how it worked; I'm gay, you're gay so let's get together. I quickly found out that there were some white women who wanted no part of me because I was black. They would make snide remarks, and give me disdainful looks like I had the plague or something. I was used to discrimination of color simply from growing up in a mostly white community, and I was also accustomed to gay intolerance, but to have both issues combined, and be subjected to them by members of my gay "family" was quite an eye-opener. I don't know what made me think that something like this would never happen.

As I said before, not all white gays are this way; my wife of three years was Caucasian, as were several of the women that I dated, but to the rest of the white gay community who thinks that they are superior to other races, I'm here to tell you that you need a serious reality check. God created us all in His image, and He is the Father of each and every one of us. So whatever race, creed or color God is, we are all of the same breed, sons and daughters of God through Jesus Christ.

Being a gay Christian is a sensitive subject within the church and society. The conservative Christians can't seem to put a finger on how homosexuality and Christianity blend together. Even non-Christians who know nothing about Christianity ponder the likelihood of how such a thing could be possible. It's almost as though these individuals are telling the gay community that we have no right to love Jesus Christ and accept Him as our Savior. The choice is ours to make; we have the privilege to let Jesus into our lives and praise and worship Him as much as we want. No one can take that away.

By taking advantage of God's Precious Gift to us, we are guaranteed a place in The Kingdom that has been prepared for us in eternity. No matter who you are or what you do, as long as you have confessed that Jesus is the Son of God that died and lived again to wash away our sins, God will welcome you into Heaven with open arms. It really makes me shudder when I hear conformists say just the opposite.

Another shocking thing are the issues concerning Holy Communion; who is "allowed" to participate, and who is not. Communion is the reenactment of the Last Supper, the breaking of bread and the drinking of wine to simulate the body and the blood of Christ. Jesus broke bread and drank wine with His disciples before His crucifixion, telling them to remember Him each time they partook. This custom was passed down through the ages for all Christians that want to remember the blood that Jesus shed for us, and His body that He unselfishly surrendered to save us from our sins. Given these facts, there are still some churches and church members that try to deny people of the tradition created by Jesus Christ. Their reasons are absurd. In one instance, a member of the congregation at my Baptist church had the audacity to tell my sister-in-law that she should not take Communion because she was not a member of the church. Another situation made national news, when a Methodist minister was defrocked for admitting that she was a lesbian, and her church revoked her rights to participate in baptisms and Communion. How can a church take away someone's right to remember the sacrifice of Jesus; what does being a member or being homosexual have to do with the sacrament of Holy Communion? As our minister at the Baptist church proclaimed to the congregation after hearing about the idiotic views of one member, "Communion is for anyone who believes that Jesus' body was broken and battered, and His blood was poured out to cover a multitude of sins." It could not have been said any better than this; plain and simple, there are no other specific requirements to partake in the Lord's Supper. Jesus did not refuse Judas whom He knew would betray Him, and He did not turn away Peter who would ultimately deny Jesus three times, so there should not be a single soul who is unwelcome at the Lord's Table.

# Part 3

I was once asked that if Jesus returned to take back His Kingdom today, did I think that He would include me. My answer was quick and confidently, "Yes." Surely not because I'm perfect, because no one will ever be perfect, but merely because I feel that I have a personal relationship with Him, and I do trust my life to His merciful lovingkindness. I've entrusted Him as my Lord and Savior, and I know that He died to save me from eternity in Hell. Being a lesbian does not make me fearful of God's wrath; the fear that I have of God is respectful in nature as it should be for all of His children. God has not set out to punish His own, but to love and forgive them for their transgressions. The only ones who will suffer the wrath of God on Judgment Day are the non-believers, and even they will be given one final chance to accept Jesus Christ as their Savior.

Even when I was a heavy drinker hanging out in bars all the time, I knew that Jesus would come to that bar to get me when He made His return. Fortunately, I no longer drink alcohol so this would not be an issue anymore; this was one of many vices that God saw fit to remove from my life. He has mysteriously moved through me and done some amazing things that I am most thankful for. One of the main things was leading me to an understanding of Himself, and an understanding of my own being. The self-acceptance that He gave me led me into a life of security and tranquility. I'm not the same person that I used to be; the one who was always on edge, worried and stressed out, is now relaxed, at ease, and self-assured through God.

The difference between being self-assured through God, and being self-assured through one's self, is that if your assurance is through God then you boast about Him, and if your assurance is through yourself then you boast about you. The latter is very discourteous to God because He is the only one worthy of praise. If we talk more about God than ourselves, His blessings will be poured out upon us abundantly. Some Christians don't realize this, and all they do is inflate their own egos; thus causing God to become jealous, and take away from their spiritual prosperity.

I pray to God daily and have genuine conversations with Him, not because there is something that I need or want, but because I want Him to know that He is the center of my life. I spend most of my time in prayer thanking Him for all that He has done. God has opened windows of opportunity for me on my job and in my finances. There was one point in time that I almost lost my home due to a bad marriage that drained me financially, but God stepped in and pulled that part of my life back together; He saved my home.

One thing about God is that He works on His schedule not ours. You might pray for something for years, but God will answer it in His own time. As the old saying goes, "God may not come when you want Him to, but He's always right on time". This is so true. Sometimes He will make us wait until it feels as though we're about to crash face first into a brick wall, but in a split second He will throw a cushion up in front of us, and when we hit that wall the impact is softened one hundred times over. God will snatch us back from the very depths of destruction if we allow Him to act according to His will, and in His own time frame. There's no need in trying to rush God because He just doesn't work that way. Everything will fall into place as He sees fit.

Our Heavenly Father also has a keen sense of humor. He has blessed me with the gift of being able to make people laugh; I believe that this is one of God's purposes for me. I enjoy humoring my family, my friends, and my colleagues, or anyone who needs a good laugh. My reason for touching on this point is because one of my favorite jokes is about God. I always viewed God's people, myself included, as tiny game pieces on a huge game board with The Almighty sitting at the helm and moving us all around in the direction that He thinks we should go. I picture all the little human game pieces trying to cheat and move themselves in other directions apart from God's will, but each and every time, we lose the game and God wins. The good thing about it though, is that a win for God, is a win for us; as long as we let Him move us around on the path that He wants, we will never lose. There are some people out there who will defy my theory, and believe that they have control over their own lives, but God created us and it is He who is in charge. Some folks actually take credit for everything thing they have, such as their jobs, families, money, and their homes; never realizing that if it were not for God, they would have nothing.

There is an insurmountable peace of mind that comes when "we let go and let God".

The turning point for me was letting go of my fears, denials, and lack of self-acceptance, and letting God conquer these battles for me. Accepting my sexual orientation as a natural part of my life gave me newfound freedom and courage to not be afraid anymore, or to let society keep me locked up inside "the closet" for the rest of my life.

I hope that anyone who is struggling with how to be Christian and gay at the same time will benefit from my story. The most important thing that individuals battling with this issue must do, is first understand and believe that God loves you. You must also have faith that God created all things, and He made no mistakes in doing so. Therefore if you are gay, then it was not by accident that you were created this way. God intentionally shaped and formed you to His liking, and He has a purpose for your life. Do not let anyone cause you to miss the blessings that God has in store for you when you accept His only Son as your Savior. You have nothing to lose by surrendering your life to Him, but you'll face losing everything if you don't.

By no means am I a holy roller or a religious fanatic, I just plain and simply love God and all that He stands for. I also refuse to let anyone tell me that it is impossible for me to be gay and love God the way I do. No one could possibly know my feelings and the spiritual connection that I have with my Heavenly Father. Many times I will sit and talk to God as if He is seated right beside me; sometimes I'm praying and other times I'm praising, but no matter which it is, I know He hears every word. This is what makes my spiritual relationship so wonderful, to know that I'm never alone as long as I know God.

Concerning being alone, let's not confuse this with being lonely; there is a huge difference. For instance, since I am now living single by choice, I spend a lot of time alone with God, but I am not lonely. I truly enjoy my solitude, and in no way do I yearn for a companion at this time. I believe that God has called me into a life of celibacy and solitariness for the time being just so I can get to know Him better. I find it quite peaceful and relaxing to share my life with God, my family and a few select friends. When I was younger I used to think that my life had to revolve around relationships; that I had to constantly have a partner to make me whole. I understand now that it is not necessary to be involved with someone every moment of my life. God has humbled me and made me realize that I am a complete person in Him. I don't need someone to go to sleep with or to be there when I wake up in the morning; I can comfortably have a quiet meal by myself, go to a movie, take a long walk, and even enjoy a night on the town in the company of only me. I don't plan on being alone forever, but right now it's just what I need; of course there's always the possibility that God doesn't intend for me to meet someone to share my life with. After all, not everyone is called upon by God to be married or involved in a long-term relationship, so if this happens to be His plan for me, I'm more than honored to abide by His wishes.

Codependency is not a healthy quality to possess. In many ways it shows a sign of insecurity in the individual who manifests it. God created us to be strong-willed and stable-minded human beings, only having a dependency on Him when we do succumb to diffidence and weakness.

It's extremely odd how my relationships with men made me the codependent partner, and my relationships with women were completely the opposite. I tended to cling to the men in my life, not wanting them to make a single move unless I was able to move with them. I guess it was a sense of insecurity that I felt with men that I did not have with women. It seems that the women I dated and had relationships with, all had that same level of insecurity, always wanting me to be near them, and not allowing me to have my space and personal time that I needed for myself.

Maybe it's a "woman thing", because I was the dominant figure in my lesbian relationships and the ladies sensed this characteristic within me, whereas the men were the dominant ones in my counterfeit hetero unions. Whatever the case may be, my point is basically this, God is the only one that we need to cling to for stability, security and reliance; no woman or man can provide this for us on a constant basis.

Speaking of dominance in lesbian relationships, our society tends to assume that there is a "male" figure within the confines of lesbian love. I'll never forget when I "came out" to my mother in a four-page letter, the first thing she said when we finally talked face to face was, "I thought I had a daughter, not a son." I explained to her that she still did have a daughter, but her daughter was a lesbian. I also told her about the woman in my life at that time, and her next response was, "Well, I don't understand. Which one of you is the man?" Once again I told her that I was a woman, and my partner was also a woman, neither of us were men, nor trying to be men. This was the hardest part for my mother to comprehend; it is also the most difficult for the majority of our society to understand. I consider myself a dominant woman, not butch, just dominant. I get very disgusted when labels are affixed to the gay community, not just by outsiders, but also by our own "family" of gay people. There are actually some feminine lesbians who will only date hard butch women, aka "studs". On the other hand there are many "studs" that will only date "femmes". I personally, am stuck somewhere in the middle between the two. I am neither "stud", nor "femme"; I'm merely dominant. So exactly what does this mean? Well, to put it into words, I would be the one in a lesbian relationship that would open doors for my mate, help her with her coat, cut the grass, and offer to pick up the tab at dinner, etc. In contrast, I also would cook up a lavish dinner, clean the house, and get the children ready for school. Believe it or not, the "stud" women would frown upon the "manly" things that I do around the house, and the "femme" women would envy the "lady-like" things. This leaves me in a sore position for being able to find a suitable mate; it's almost another form of discrimination within the gay community. It's just another instance where simply being yourself is not good enough.

As I said before, homosexuality has very little to do with "sex"; of all the things that I described as being part of a lesbian relationship, not one had to do with intercourse. Naturally, sex is involved, but it's not to the extent that society and conservative church folk lead us to believe. I'll touch upon this subject briefly. In the "stud"- "femme" relationship, the "stud" is usually the one who is the aggressor while the "femme" is submissive. Most "studs" would be highly offended if they were asked to play the submissive role. As for the "in-betweeners", we tend to be comfortable as both the aggressor and the submissive partner.

There is still no need to feel ashamed about sex even if it is with your same-sex mate. This pleasurable act of intimacy was also created by God to be shared between loving couples; using it inappropriately is the only time we should feel any type of guilt or shame, and even then we shouldn't dwell on it forever, just ask for God's forgiveness and move on. By using sex in an inappropriate way, I'm referring to lusting, adultery, and non-committed sexual relations, whether they are same-sex or opposite-sex couples that are involved.

Growing up gay in America is not an easy or deliberate task; it requires a huge amount of courage within one's self, and acceptance from those who believe that gays would intentionally choose to live a life that subjects them to discrimination, disparagement, physical abuse and even the risk of being murdered. Some members of the gay community have even committed suicide due to society's intolerance, and their own inability to understand why they cannot be heterosexual no matter how hard they try.

Although I have not encountered any negative reactions since "coming out" in 1998, I still lived a life of fear and confusion because of the probability of being ridiculed prior to that time. I know that a time may come when I will be subjected to the ignorance of our world, but for the most part I am thankful that people have become a little more tolerant, yet still there is a long road ahead for total acceptance. Had it not been for God opening my eyes to the fact that His love is unconditional, I would probably still be living a life of torment and deceit. I pray that more of my gay brothers and sisters will also turn to God for the serenity and the courage that only He can provide. Suicide, drugs, faked heterosexuality, and self-hatred are not the answers to escape gay sexual orientation; these things only cause undue misery and anguish.

Take pride in what God created you to be. Do not be ashamed or guilt-ridden; Jesus loves you. Also, don't be afraid to be a Christian. Whenever I ask other gays if they are Christian, you wouldn't believe the look of horror that appears on their faces; it's as if they had just watched one of the scariest scenes from a Stephen King movie. I know that the panic-stricken look is because they feel they have no right to be called a child of God, but they could never be more mistaken. God is always willing to accept His own creation; we just have to be willing to accept Him into our hearts and minds. I truly think that many gays want to be Christian, but the fear of condemnation that we are misled to believe awaits us on Judgment Day deters most from making the commitment to Christ.

To this I'll say, don't let society make you turn your back on the only One who will always be there for you. The only way Jesus will deny you is if you deny Him first. Why take that kind of gamble with where you will spend eternity? It's so much easier if you just claim Jesus as your own. He is there waiting for every one of us to accept Him into our lives, to put Him in the center of our everyday existence. The transformation that would take place inside if you only let Jesus in is so awe-inspiring it's virtually unexplainable. I've tried my best to put it into words in this writing, but it's still something that you'd have to experience to get the true feeling, the true essence, the true meaning of what I'm trying to say.

I had a friend who once told me that he would not go to church because people could tell he was gay by looking at him and he was ashamed. He said he didn't want anyone to single him out and question him about why a gay man would come to church. I promptly told him that this was nonsense and he had just as much right to be in God's house as anyone else. I also told him that he should not let "people" interfere with his desire to worship God publicly because none of them would be willing to answer to God for him in the end. It really irked me that my friend would allow these people to hinder his relationship with God. We just can't let others pave our way to Hell; we've got to stand firm in our belief and disregard their ignorance.

Jesus said, *"For God so loved the world that He gave His only begotten Son; that 'whosoever' believeth in Him should not perish, but have everlasting life."* (John 3:16.)

*"Whosoever"* believeth. The Lord Jesus Christ said "whosoever". The last time I checked, whosoever meant "everybody", and everybody means "all". All includes every single person whether gay, lesbian, bisexual, transgendered, straight, any race, creed or color. It means "everybody". So if Jesus had any restrictions I'm sure He would have stated them, but He didn't. We are all welcome in God's Kingdom.

Just as Jesus had no limitations on who could have everlasting life through His saving grace, He also did not mention one word about homosexuality in His preaching, (as I stated previously in Part 1 of this book). None of the gospels touch upon this issue in any way. The apostle Paul gave his own theory in Romans regarding what many deem as God's disapproval of homosexuality. Paul wrote in a letter to the Romans about their idolatry and dishonoring of God by worshipping birds, four-footed animals, and crawling creatures. Thus God became angry and gave them over to "degrading passions" where the women exchanged unnatural acts with each other, and the men abandoned their natural function with women and burned in desire for one another. (Romans 1: 23-27). This appears to be God's punishment for the idolaters who were obviously heterosexual; he allowed them to do what was "unnatural" for them; just as is would be "unnatural" for a homosexual to become or try to become "straight".

By no means am I a theologian, but I have read the entire Bible cover to cover, and I'm not convinced that being born homosexual is immoral. I sincerely believe that Jesus would have told us in no uncertain terms that homosexuality is a sin. Therefore, it would behoove everyone who has a fear of condemnation to face the reality that God is a loving God, full of grace, mercy and acceptance. He will only condemn those who reject Jesus Christ as the Savior.

My personal goal is to bring as many gays as I can to Christ, especially those who are only separated from Him because of the issues concerning their orientation. The majority of us are not gay because we want to be, but we are gay by predestination. All one has to do is simply ask yourself, "Why? Why would anyone deliberately choose to live such a life of controversy that could bring harm, ridicule or death?"

This is my belief due to my own personal experience as I tried to change how God created me through nearly two decades of deceiving, denying, hiding, and being ashamed. Trying to undo God's will for my life only caused me sorrow and pain. It took a long time for me to realize that the One I was running from was the only One who could save me.

To sum it all up, let's just imagine what it would be like to spend twenty years living as someone other than yourself. Envision being so afraid of society's ignorant opinions that you would jump into a marriage even if you didn't want to be married; concoct lie after lie about your true feelings, and feel so ashamed of your own sexual identity that you would consider suicide, or maybe even follow through with it. This isn't a very pretty picture; it's a torturous way to have to live. No one would truly understand unless they have personally endured it.

The only guaranteed way out of this turmoil and strife is to know The Lord; and if my story helps even one person find God, then I will have accomplished something. Remember, don't ensue the battle all by yourself; recruit Jesus the Christ to be your Leader.

The End

# About the Author

I was born in 1963 in a small town in Western Pennsylvania called New Castle. My passion for writing began there nearly 25 years ago when my 12th grade English teacher, Mr. Robert Craig, took notice of my creative writing ability, and submitted a poem that I had written entitled *A Positive State of Mind* to the National Poetry Press, Agoura, CA in 1981. That was my first and only publication. After graduating from New Castle Senior High School, I moved to Pittsburgh, PA (my home for the past 21 years) and dabbled with writing short stories from time to time. Instead of pursuing my dream of becoming a well-known author, I got married at a young age, had one child, and became sidetracked by all the duties and responsibilities expected of a mother and wife.

During most of my life I struggled with issues concerning my own sexual orientation, but never had the courage to face the demons publicly. By the time I was 27, I found myself a divorced, confused, single mother, still in denial regarding my desire for same-sex relationships. It wasn't until 8 years later that God finally led me to a life of self-acceptance.

By 2004, I found myself aspiring to continue with my writing, and to create a story that others in my situation could relate to, so I began to pick up where I left off 25 years ago with my hopes of becoming a well-known author. God has helped me realize that it's never too late to cash in on a dream.

www.ingramcontent.com/pod-product-compliance
Lightning Source LLC
Chambersburg PA
CBHW031330290526
45784CB00014B/2458